DANIEL'S DATA

This data belongs to

Tamsin

part of **Space Academy** at

St. Olaf's

First published 2012
ISBN 978 1 84427 708 7

Scripture Union
207–209 Queensway
Bletchley
Milton Keynes
MK2 2EB
email: info@scriptureunion.org.uk
www.scriptureunion.org.uk

British Library Cataloguing-in-Publication Data

A catalogue record of this book is available from the British Library.

Printed and bound in Singapore by Tien Wah Press

Cover and internal design by kwgraphicdesign

Cover illustration by Sean Parkes

Internal illustration by Sean Parkes

Scripture Union is an international Christian charity working with churches in more than 130 countries.

Thank you for purchasing this book. Any profits from this book support SU in England and Wales to bring the good news of Jesus Christ to children, young people and families and to enable them to meet God through the Bible and prayer.

Find out more about our work and how you can get involved at:
www.scriptureunion.org.uk (England and Wales)
www.suscotland.org.uk (Scotland)
www.suni.co.uk (Northern Ireland)
www.scriptureunion.org (USA)
www.su.org.au (Australia)

Copies of the CEV Bible can be purchased from www.bibleresources.org.uk

Welcome to Daniel's Data.

In these pages, you'll be joining Daniel in an amazing adventure where he has to make difficult choices, combat enemies, understand dreams, and do impossible things, all the time living boldly for God in a world that does not even know God exists!

Debug the data, solve the puzzles, avoid the lions, get the signatures of your Astronaut friends and discover how you can trust God like Daniel did! Here, you'll also find bits of the Bible to help you discover what it means to follow God, to live boldly for him – and to have confidence in God's power!

The Bible is split into two sections (the Old Testament and the New Testament).

These two sections are split into books (the Old Testament has 39 books, the New Testament has 27). The books are split into chapters (the biggest book, Psalms, has 150 chapters!) and those chapters are split into verses (the longest chapter is Psalm 119 with 176 verses!). Sometimes you'll see a Bible verse written like this: **Daniel 1:8**. Here is how you tell which verse to read:

Daniel 1 : 8

Daniel means we need to look for the Bible book of Daniel. If you are not sure where this is, look for the contents page near the beginning of the Bible.

1 means we need to look for the big number 1; we call it chapter 1.

8 means we need to look for the little number 8; we call it verse 8.

Debug your data!

Here and there, you may find star-dust has got into **Daniel's Data**, and corrupted the files. Use this page to find a tech-fix to debug the data.

Space-fix codebreaker

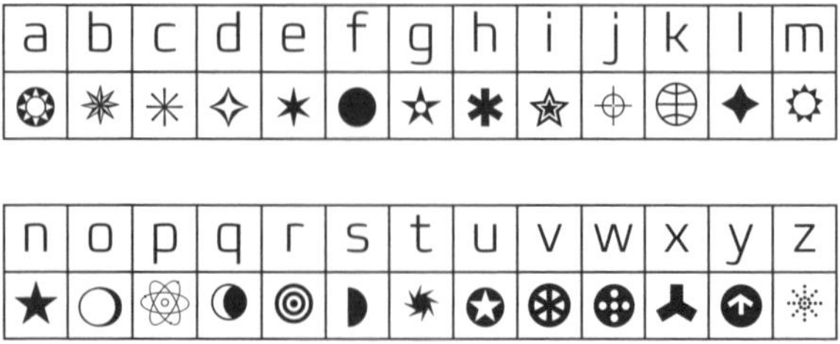
a b c d e f g h i j k l m
n o p q r s t u v w x y z

Tech-fix codebreaker

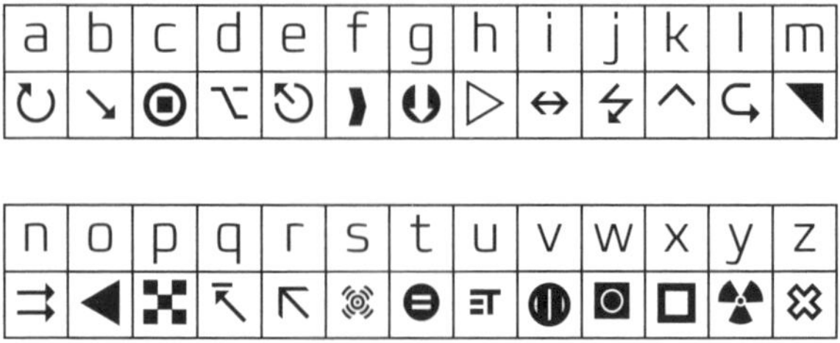
a b c d e f g h i j k l m
n o p q r s t u v w x y z

Try tech-fixing the Space Academy Learn and remember verse.

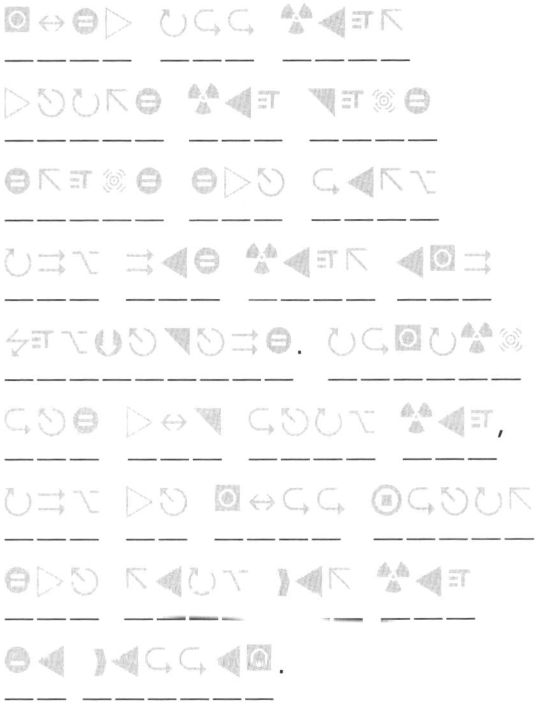

Proverbs 3:5,6

Forbidden food

To a different world

Daniel and his friends lived in Jerusalem until King Nebuchadnezzar came, captured the city and took them to live in Babylon, 800 km away. They followed the trading routes of the day. These were not straight so they would have travelled more like 1,600 km.

Try and work out the way they went, on this map:

Euphrates
Jordan
Dead Sea
Jerusalem
START

A long way from home

For Daniel and his friends, everything was so different in Babylon. Different way of speaking. Different food. Different type of house. Even a different type of school! Almost like being on a different planet!

What would you miss most if you were taken away from your home? Write or draw it here.

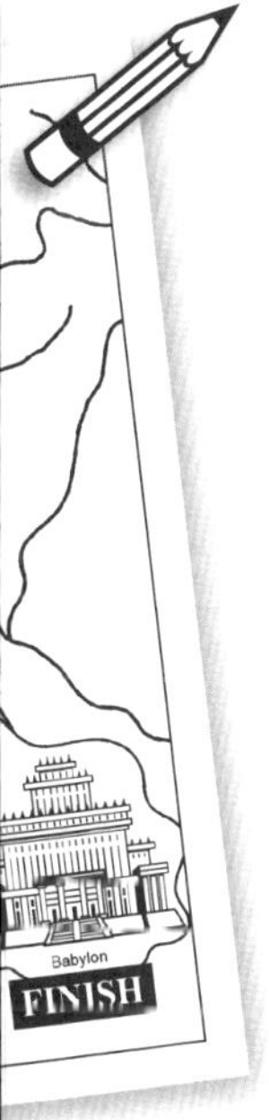
Babylon
FINISH

VOYAGE 1

Where would, or could, you be, if you were taken 800 km from home?

Daniel's diet

King Nebuchadnezzar provided lots of lovely food (or so he thought) but Daniel and his friends asked to eat only vegetables. It wasn't because they'd decided to be vegetarians.

Read about it from the Bible and see if you can work out why. Underline the words that tell you the reason.

Daniel 1:8–14

8 Daniel made up his mind to eat and drink only
what God had approved for his people to eat. And
he asked the king's chief official for permission not
to eat the food and wine served in the royal palace. 9
God had made the official friendly and kind to Daniel.
10 But the man still told him, "The king has decided
what you must eat and drink. And I am afraid he will
kill me, if you eat something else and end up looking
worse than the other young men."

11 The king's official had put a guard in charge of
Daniel and his three friends. So Daniel said to the
guard, 12 "For the next ten days, let us have only
vegetables and water at mealtime. 13 When the ten
days are up, compare how we look with the other
young men, and decide what to do with us."

14 The guard agreed to do what Daniel had asked.

What happened next?

Colour in or circle the answer.

The guard was worried that...

Daniel trusted God that...

What do you think will happen?
Write or draw your answer here.

Turn the page to find out...

Ten days later

Daniel 1:15,16

15 Ten days later, Daniel and his friends looked
healthier and better than the young men who had
been served food from the royal palace.

16 After this, the guard let them eat vegetables instead
of the rich food and wine.

Is that what you thought would happen?

Why – or why not? What *did* you expect?

Food for thought

The Bible tells us that Daniel and his friends were chosen by the palace official to be trained to become court officials. But, oh no! The star-dust has corrupted the file! Go to page 4 to find a tech-fix to debug the data.

Daniel 1:17–21

[17] God made the four young men _ _ _ _ _
and _ _ _ _. They read a lot of
_ _ _ _ _ and became well educated. Daniel
could also tell the meaning of _ _ _ _ _ _
and visions.

[18] At the end of the three-year period set by King
Nebuchadnezzar, his chief palace official brought
all the young men to him. [19] The king interviewed
them and discovered that none of the others
were as _ _ _ _ _ _ _ _ _ _ _
as Daniel, Hananiah, Mishael, and Azariah.
So they were given positions in the royal
_ _ _ _ _. [20] From then on, whenever the
king asked for _ _ _ _ _ _, he found
their _ _ _ _ _ _ was _ _ _ times
_ _ _ _ _ _ than that of any of his other
advisors and magicians. [21] Daniel served there until
the first year of King Cyrus.

You'll hear about Hananiah, Mishael, and Azariah again in Voyage 3, using the names they were given in Babylon: Shadrach, Meshach and Abednego

Data capture

Daniel, Shadrach, Meshach and Abednego chose to stand firm for God and follow his ways. It may not *seem* very important – it was just about what they ate – but it was a risky thing to do, for them and for their guard. They chose God's way and God did not let them down.

What does this tell you about God?

How do you feel after hearing this?

Do you think God will help you, when you think about what he wants you to do and do your best to live his way?

How might he help?

Remember you can talk with your ***Space Academy*** leader about it.

Talk with God

What does God want to say to you today?

What do you want to say to God?

Difficult dream

Sleepless nights

Can you remember any of your dreams? Were they happy dreams – or nightmares? King Nebuchadnezzar of Babylon had a bad dream – and he took drastic action! Find out more here...

Daniel 2:1–6

1 During the second year that Nebuchadnezzar was
king, he had such horrible nightmares that he could
not sleep. 2 So he called in his counsellors, advisors,
magicians, and wise men, 3 and said, "I am disturbed
by a dream that I don't understand, and I want you to
explain it."

4 They answered in Aramaic, "Your Majesty, we hope
you live forever! We are your servants. Please tell us
your dream, and we will explain what it means."

5 But the king replied, "No! I have made up my mind.
If you don't tell me both the dream and its meaning,
you will be chopped to pieces and your houses will
be torn down. 6 However, if you do tell me both the
dream and its meaning, you will be greatly rewarded
and highly honoured. Now tell me the dream and
explain what it means."

Circle the words that describe the dream.

Can't do it? Nor could the king's advisers! Look again at verse 5 and see what the king says he will do to them.

What would it be like?

Imagine you are going to be punished for something you haven't done. Draw your face on the head-shape. Draw thought-bubbles around the words that you are thinking. Write more thoughts in the empty bubbles.

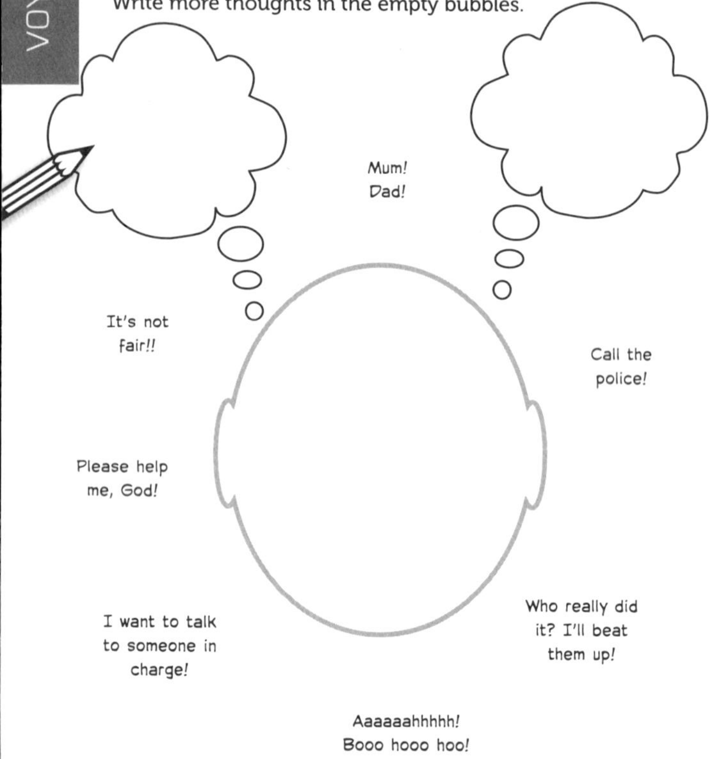
Mum!
Dad!
It's not fair!!
Call the police!
Please help me, God!
I want to talk to someone in charge!
Who really did it? I'll beat them up!
Aaaaaahhhhh!
Booo hooo hoo!

It's not fair!

Do you think King Nebuchadnezzar was being fair? His advisers protested! How could they explain the dream when they didn't know what it was?

Daniel 2:12–19

12,13 This made the king so angry that he gave orders for every wise man in Babylonia to be put to death, including Daniel and his three friends.

14 Arioch was the king's official in charge of putting
the wise men to death. He was on his way to have
it done, when Daniel very wisely went to him 15 and
asked, "Why did the king give such cruel orders?"

After Arioch explained what had happened, 16 Daniel
rushed off and said to the king, "If you will just give me some time, I'll explain your dream."

17 Daniel returned home and told his three friends.
18 Then he said, "Pray that the God who rules from heaven will be merciful and explain this mystery, so that we and the others won't be put to death."

19 In a vision one night, Daniel was shown the dream and its meaning. Then he praised the God who rules from heaven.

Who did Daniel speak to? Circle them all.
Underline what he said.

How did he know the dream and its meaning?

Cross words!

The king was so ***angry*** that we have a ***cross***word for this data. Work out the clues and then find the hidden word.

All clues work 'across' the puzzle.

1 The king was going to punish his advisers with... ? [5 letters]

2 Daniel asked his three friends to... ? [4 letters]

3 Who asked the king for more time? [6 letters]

4 After God gave Daniel the answer, his friends _______ God [7 letters]

5 The king planned to kill his what? [4 and 3 letters]

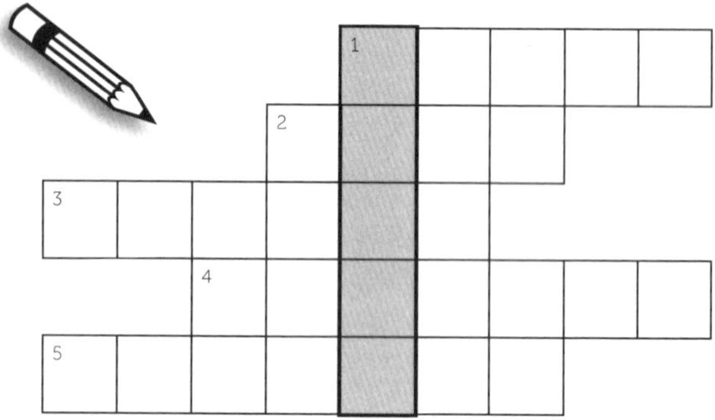
1
2
3
4
5

Find the answers on page 19.

Daniel explains

God told Daniel about the dream and Daniel described it to the king. There was an enormous statue made, from top to bottom, of gold, silver, bronze, iron and a mix of iron and clay. A huge stone knocked the statue down – and then the stone became a mountain!

Then Daniel explained the meaning:

Daniel 2:37–39a

37 Your Majesty, you are the greatest of kings, and
God has highly honoured you with power 38 over all
humans, animals, and birds. You are the head of gold.
39 After you are gone, another kingdom will rule, but it
won't be as strong.

Daniel explained that this next kingdom, and others that came after it, would all come to an end, until ...

Daniel 2:44,45

44–45 ... the God who rules from heaven will set up an
eternal kingdom that will never fall. It will be like the
stone ... that crushed the iron, bronze, clay, silver, and
gold. Your Majesty, in your dream the great God has
told you what is going to happen, and you can trust
this interpretation.

VOYAGE 2

Draw the king's face at different times in the story:

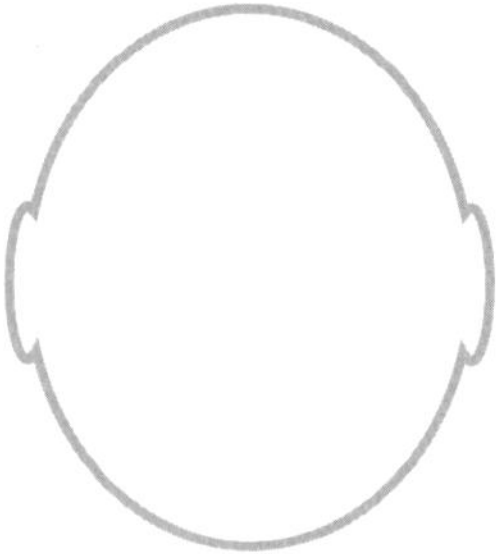

When he had the dream.

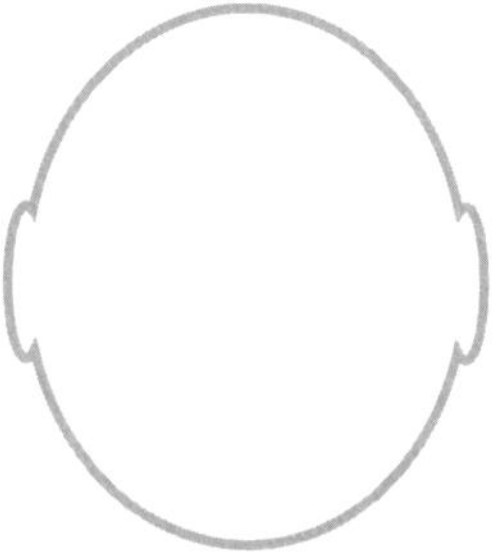

When the wise men couldn't tell it to him.

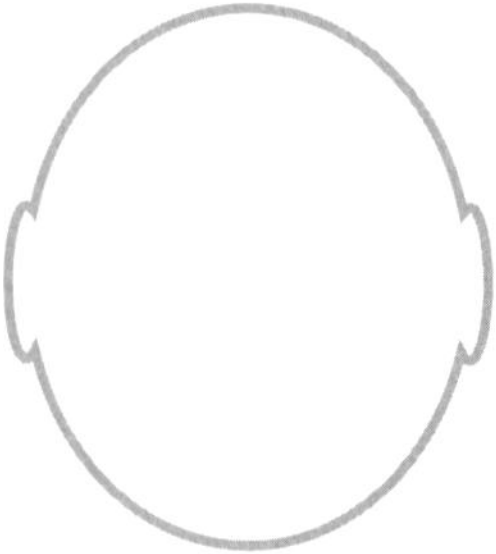

When Daniel asked for more time.

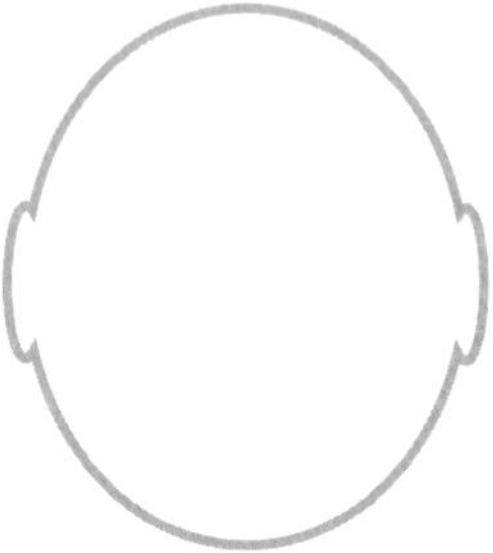

When Daniel told the king the dream.

God made it possible for Daniel to do something no one else could do. The king was so pleased with Daniel that he made him his chief adviser and gave important jobs to his three friends.

Data capture

Daniel had to do something impossible or he and his friends would be killed! He promised to tell the king about the dream even before he knew what it was. He must have really trusted that God would help him.

Is there anything that really worries you, or makes you afraid? Are there things that seem impossible? God will help you with it: you can trust him, like Daniel did.

Right at the end of the king's dream, he saw a great stone that broke the statue, without anyone touching it. Daniel explained that this would be a kingdom that would never end, set up by the God of heaven. Christians believe this kingdom began when Jesus came to earth (a long time after Daniel lived). Find out more on page 43.

Talk with God

Thank God that he helped Daniel to be brave and go to the king.

Praise God that he told Daniel the dream in the night.

Ask God to help you with the things that seem impossible to you.

answers to ***cross***word puzzle on page 16
1 death; **2** pray; **3** Daniel; **4** praised; **5** wise men **hidden word**: dream

Stunning statue

Work it out

King Nebuchadnezzar seemed to get statues on the brain. Perhaps it was the dream that he had, which Daniel had explained to him. Whatever it was, Nebuchadnezzar had a giant statue made. It was 27 metres high and 3 metres wide!

How tall are you? If you are in a group, how tall are the others? Try to work out how many of you standing one on top of each other you would need to be 27 metres high.

It would take ____ children my size to be as high as King Nebuchadnezzar's statue.

If you lie on the ground, how many of you would you need to be 3 metres wide?

It would take ____ children my size lying on the ground to be as wide as King Nebuchadnezzar's statue.

Ask your friends to lie on the floor in a circle that is 3 metres wide, to give you an idea of how big the base of the statue would be. You'll need plenty of space!

27m high
3m
wide

King's command

The statue wasn't just for looking at.

Read about it here; then underline the words of the king's command. Circle the words that say what will happen if anyone disobeys.

Daniel 3:1–7

1 King Nebuchadnezzar ordered a gold statue to be
built ninety feet high and nine feet wide. He had it
set up in Dura Valley near the city of Babylon, 2 and
he commanded his governors, advisors, treasurers,
judges, and his other officials to come from
everywhere in his kingdom to the dedication of the
statue. 3 So all of them came and stood in front of it.

4 Then an official stood up and announced:

"People of every nation and race, now listen to
the king's command! 5 Trumpets, flutes, harps,
and all other kinds of musical instruments will
soon start playing. When you hear the music, you
must bow down and worship the statue that King
Nebuchadnezzar has set up. 6 Anyone who refuses
will at once be thrown into a flaming furnace."

7 As soon as the people heard the music, they bowed
down and worshipped the gold statue that the king
had set up.

We still won't!

... well not quite everyone bowed down.

Remember Shadrach, Meshach and Abednego (Daniel's three friends)? They did not worship the statue. The king gave them one more chance but here's what the Bible says they did:

It sounds as if that's the end of Shadrach, Meshach and Abednego. What do you think will happen next?

Daniel 3:16–23

16 The three men replied, "Your Majesty, we don't
need to defend ourselves.
17 The God we worship can
save us from you and your flaming furnace.
18 But even if he doesn't, we still won't worship your
gods and the gold statue you have set up."

19 Nebuchadnezzar's face twisted with anger at
the three men. And he ordered the furnace to be
heated seven times hotter than usual.
20 Next, he
commanded some of his strongest soldiers to tie up
the men and throw them into the flaming furnace.
21-23 The king wanted it done at that very moment.
So the soldiers tied up Shadrach, Meshach, and
Abednego and threw them into the flaming furnace
with all of their clothes still on, including their
turbans. The fire was so hot that flames leaped out
and killed the soldiers.

Debug the data

Get your space-fix from page 4.

The king's order was clear, when you hear the

_ _ _ _ _ you must _ _ _ _ _ _ _

and _ _ _ _ _ _ _ the statue.

The three friends were clear too. The _ _ _ we

_ _ _ _ _ _ _ can _ _ _ _ us from

_ _ _ and your _ _ _ _ _ _ _

_ _ _ _ _ _ _. But even if he doesn't we still

_ _ _'_ _ _ _ _ _ _ _ the statue.

That's a real wow!! That's truly trusting God and worshipping only him. That's amazing!

Power prayers

Draw lots of flames to fill the flaming furnace. Write the name of someone you would like to pray for on each flame – especially anyone who needs God's help and power! It can be anyone: a friend, someone in your family, and people you don't know like children who are hungry, or scared, or in a country with a war going on.

What do you want to say to God about the people on your flames?

What happened next!

Shadrach, Meshach and Abednego are in the hot furnace. What will God do about it? Here's a bit more from the Bible.

Daniel 3:24–28

24 Suddenly the king jumped up and shouted, "Weren't only three men tied up and thrown into the fire?"

"Yes, Your Majesty," the people answered.

25 "But I see four men walking around in the fire," the king replied. "None of them is tied up or harmed, and the fourth one looks like a god."

26 Nebuchadnezzar went closer to the flaming furnace and said to the three young men, "You servants of the Most High God, come out at once!"
They came out, 27 and the king's high officials,
governors, and advisors all crowded around them. The men were not burned, their hair wasn't scorched, and their clothes didn't even smell like smoke.

28 King Nebuchadnezzar said: Praise their God for sending an angel to rescue his servants! They trusted their God and refused to obey my commands. Yes, they chose to die rather than to worship or serve any god except their own.

Draw a circle round the words that you think are most 'Wow!'

Underline anything that does not make sense to you: talk about it with your *Space Academy* leader.

Data capture

It was not easy or safe living God's way in Babylon! Shadrach, Meshach and Abednego have obeyed God about what to eat. Now they have a much greater test: this time they will die in a horrible way if they stand firm for God and choose to worship only him.

What are Shadrach, Meshach and Abednego like in this story? Think of three words to describe them.

What is God like in this story?

What do you think God should do?

What does he do?

When the three friends did what God wanted, he sent someone special to be with them in the furnace. Who could it have been? Look closely at Daniel 3:25 and talk with your *Space Academy* leader about who you think it was.

Talk with God

How important is God to you? Praise him for his power and tell him how you feel about this story.

Rewind

Try this quick quiz to see how much you know about Daniel already.

1 Daniel lived...

- ☐ a before Jesus.
- ☐ b after Jesus.
- ☐ c at the same time as Jesus.

2 Daniel was living in...

- ☐ a London.
- ☐ b Babylon.
- ☐ c Rome.

3 Daniel heard about God...

- ☐ a as a boy.
- ☐ b as a young man.
- ☐ c when he was an old man.

4 Daniel's people were in Babylon...

- ☐ a on holiday.
- ☐ b for trade.
- ☐ c because the Babylonians had taken them prisoner.

Answers 1 a 500 years or so; 2 b; 3 a he always knew; 4 c

The heavenly hand

Design and draw the best party ever!

King Belshazzar gave a party for 1,000 people. If you gave the biggest and best party what would you want to have? Draw your choices in the boxes.

Food

Drink

Games or Disco

Special things

A hand without an arm or a body!

At King Belshazzar's party, the drinks were served in gold and silver cups – but these were special cups that were used to worship God, in the Temple in Jerusalem. It was as though Belshazzar was laughing at God by using them. Here's what the Bible says next:

Daniel 5:5,6

5 Suddenly a human hand was seen writing on the
plaster wall of the palace. The hand was just behind
the lampstand, and the king could see it writing. 6 He
was so frightened that his face turned pale, his knees
started shaking, and his legs became weak.

No one could read the words or explain them. Now, Belshazzar was "more afraid than ever before, and his face turned white as a ghost." (verse 9)

Why did it matter that Belshazzar used the cups?

Would you have been afraid?

What do you think will happen next?

The worst party ever?

Read the full story from the Bible, in Daniel chapter 5.

Belshazzar's party was suddenly interrupted!

Draw the hand, writing on the wall.

AAAAHH!!!
OOOOOH!!
MENE MENE TEKEL PARSIN
WHAAAT?!

Add the scared Belshazzar and his guests to the picture.

Copy these words into the right speech bubbles:

- Daniel is wise. He will tell you.
- Tell me what it means.
- Send for Daniel!
- We don't know!

MENE MENE
TEKEL PARSIN

Draw Daniel coming to see the king. What does the king ask him? Add the words.

King Belshazzar, you refused to worship the God who gives you breath and controls everything you do. That's why he sent the hand to write this message on the wall.

Draw Daniel talking to the king.

The words say: 'numbered', 'weighed' and 'divided'.

Draw Daniel and the king.

What does it mean?

Now Belshazzar knew what the writing said – but he still did not know what it meant. Here's what Daniel said:

Daniel 5:28

God has numbered the days of your kingdom and has brought it to an end. He has weighed you on his balance scales, and you fall short of what it takes to be king. So God has divided your kingdom between the Medes and the Persians.

That still isn't very clear. Time to debug the data. Get a tech-fix from page 4 to help you work out the meaning.

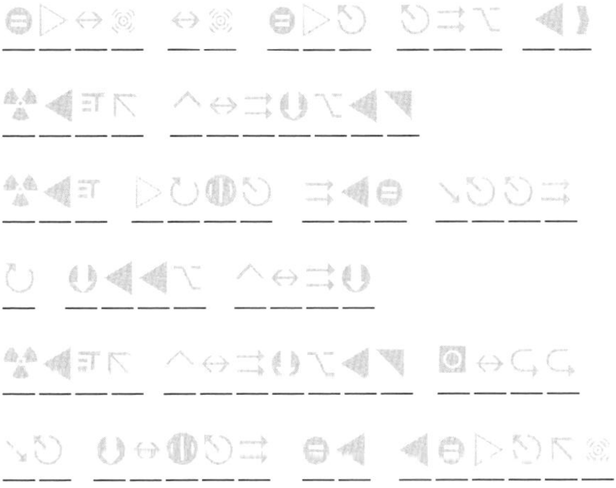

Did it come true? 

Data capture

King Belshazzar found out that God is real and powerful – and that it matters how people treat him! Some people say that it doesn't matter what we do or that God will let us off – but this story shows that God does mind.

If you want to be like Daniel, not like the king, what sort of things should you be careful about? What does God want? What doesn't God want?

If you are not sure, how could you find out?

Talk with God

Ask God to forgive you for anything that you have done which could make him angry. Thank God that he forgives us when we are sorry and tell him.

What else do you want to say to him? Say it now!

In the pit

I'm in charge!

If you were in charge of your country, what would you do? What things would you change? Write or draw pictures to show your ideas here.

Do you think you would be good at being in charge? Why – or why not?

VOYAGE 5

Daniel in charge

Daniel has been living in Babylon for about 50 years now and is working for the new king, Darius. Daniel is very good at being in charge but that is making two other officials jealous. They try to catch him doing wrong – but he always does what is right. Daniel is still living God's way and his enemies realise that this is how they will get him into trouble! Read about their plan in the Bible.

Will Daniel obey the new law?
What will happen if he doesn't?

Daniel 6:6–9

6 They all went to the king and said:

"Your Majesty, we hope you live forever! 7 All of your
officials, leaders, advisors, and governors agree that
you should make a law forbidding anyone to pray
to any god or human except you for the next thirty
days. Everyone who disobeys this law must be
thrown into a pit of lions. 8 Order this to be written
and then sign it, so it cannot be changed, just as
no written law of the Medes and Persians can be
changed."

9 So King Darius made the law and had it written
down.

Daniel prays – as always

Read this verse (Daniel 6:10) and write down five things about Daniel talking to God.

Daniel heard about the law, but when he returned home, he went upstairs and prayed in front of the window that faced Jerusalem. In the same way that he had always done, he knelt down in prayer three times a day, giving thanks to God.

1.

2.

3.

4.

5.

Do you think Daniel is... ? (circle up to 3 words)

proud
silly
brave
wise
good
lions' dinner
crazy
weak
daring
right
at risk

Daniel's ups and downs

Here's what happened next to Daniel. For each line of the story, work out whether this is good news or bad news. Add a bar to the graph.

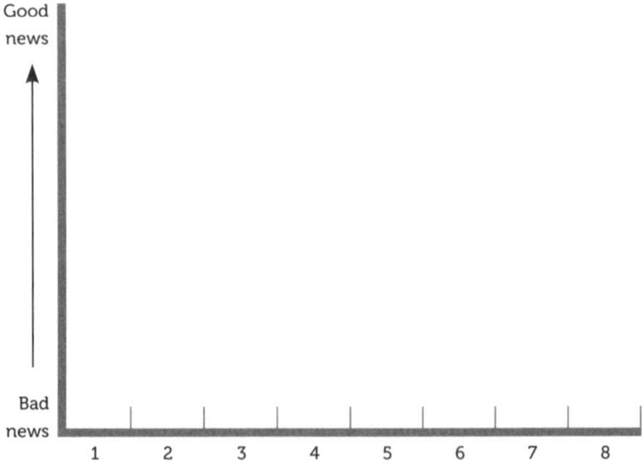
Good news
Bad news
1
2
3
4
5
6
7
8

Where have you put the last bar on your graph?
What will Darius find when the pit is opened?

1 Daniel prayed, as always.
2 His enemies saw him.
3 His enemies told the king.
4 The king did not want to have to keep the law: he tried to save Daniel.
5 The law had to be kept.
6 Daniel was thrown into a pit of lions.
7 Darius said, "You have been faithful to your God, and I pray that he will rescue you."
8 Next morning, Darius went back to the pit.

Next morning

Daniel has spent all night in the pit of lions.

King Darius has spent all night in his palace, not able to sleep because he is so worried about Daniel. Here's what the Bible tells us:

Daniel 6:19–23

19 At daybreak the king got up and ran to the pit. 20 He
was anxious and shouted, "Daniel, you were faithful
and served your God. Was he able to save you from
the lions?"

21 Daniel answered, "Your Majesty, I hope you live
forever! 22 My God knew that I was innocent, and he
sent an angel to keep the lions from eating me. Your
Majesty, I have never done anything to hurt you."

23 The king was relieved to hear Daniel's voice, and he
gave orders for him to be taken out of the pit. Daniel's
faith in his God had kept him from being harmed.

Circle the words that describe Daniel.

How many times does the name 'God' appear? Tick each time.

How and why was Daniel kept safe?

In case you're thinking the lions were just not hungry, here's verse 24: 'And the king ordered the men who had brought charges against Daniel to be thrown into the pit, together with their wives and children. But before they even reached the bottom, the lions ripped them to pieces.'

Who prays?

There has been a lot about praying in Voyage 5. Here are some praise words from Daniel chapter 6. Get your space-fix from page 4 to debug the data.

"He is the _ _ _ _ _ _ God, the one who lives _ _ _ _ _ _ _. His _ _ _ _ _ and his _ _ _ _ _ _ _ will _ _ _ _ _ _ _ _. He _ _ _ _ _ _ _ people and sets them _ _ _ _ by working great _ _ _ _ _ _ _ _."

Who do you think said this about God? _ _ _ _ _ _

Was that a surprise to you? Daniel's faith and courage meant that the king believed in God too, and wanted everyone in the country to worship him.

How many different ways of praying can you think of? Draw stick-people praying in different ways. Here is one to get you started:

Data capture

Daniel's life was full of prayer, even when facing lions. He risked his life by praying to God and God answered his prayers. God even answered the prayers of King Darius who did not believe in him at the time!

Tick the box if you agree that:

☐ Daniel was bold and brave, for God.

☐ Daniel believed in God and trusted God, whatever.

What else could you say about Daniel and God?

Tick the box if you want to say:

☐ I want to be bold and brave, for God.

☐ I want to believe in God and trust him whatever.

What else do you want to say about you and God?

Talk with God

Thank God for all that you have learnt about Daniel this week at *Space Academy*.

Ask him to help you live for him and stay close to him, as Daniel did.

Do you find it hard to do what you know God wants you to? What can you do about these hard things? Is there anyone you could talk to about them, to get some help? Maybe you could talk to your *Space Academy* leader.

Trusting God, like Daniel and his friends

Now you have found out lots about Daniel and his friends and how they trusted in God, what do you think? Circle what is closest to what you think.

I think I'm interested, but not just yet.

I would love to trust God and be like Daniel.

I am already trusting God, like Daniel and his friends.

I am not really bothered, thanks.

I try to trust in God but I need some help.

Chat to your *Space Academy* leader about want you have circled – they would love to know and to help you, if you want.

Trusting in God starts with Jesus

Daniel and his friends lived hundreds of years before Jesus was on earth so we know a lot more about Jesus than they did. For us, trusting in God starts with Jesus. Jesus came to show us what God is like and to help us trust in God. If we are worried about the things we have done wrong, Jesus came so that we can be forgiven – that's why he died on the cross and why God brought him to life again. (Ask your *Space Academy* leader to tell you more about this.) Jesus wants us to be his friends and to put our trust in him.

If you want to do that – just tell him, in your own words. If you are not sure what to say, you could use this prayer.

Lord Jesus, I want to be your friend.

Thank you that you came to earth to show us what God is like.

Thank you that you died on the cross.

I'm sorry for all the wrong things I have said or done or thought.

Please forgive me and let me be your friend.

Please may the Holy Spirit help me to be more like you.

Amen

Space Academy

My Best Bits

The **funniest** bit:

The **silliest** bit:

The bit I wanted to go on **longer**:

What I **learnt about God**:

What I will **remember most**:

What I want **to do next**:

Starbase mates

On these pages, collect the names, messages and doodles of the Astronauts in your Starbase. Remember your leaders, too!

So, who is God?

Where did God come from? How do you know you can trust God? How do you know God is your friend? Does God ever go to bed? Find out answers to these questions and more, by discovering what the Bible says about God.

£9.99

So, who is GOD?
Answers to real questions about God
Robert Willoughby

BIBLE HEROES
My book about being a hero for God
Nick Harding

Bible Heroes

Challenges, facts, puzzles – to do on your own or with your mates. Meet the men (and boys) of the Bible who stood up for God and didn't simply go along with the crowd. Find out how you can be a hero for God too!

Nick Harding **£4.99**

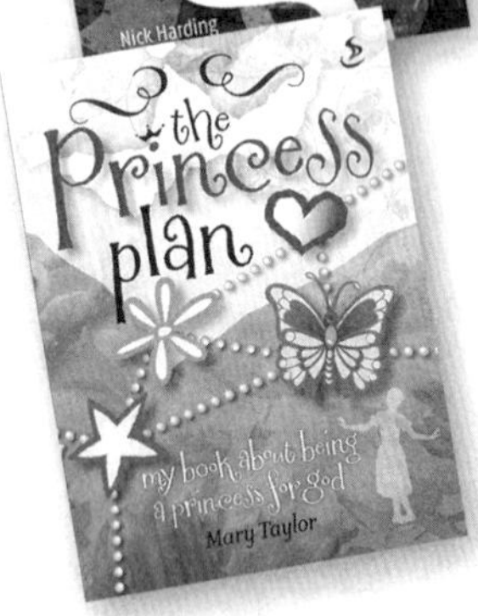
the Princess plan
my book about being a princess for god
Mary Taylor

Princess Plan

If you always thought you were born to be a princess, this scrapbook is for you! Fun things to make, do and read about girls and women from the Bible who were special to God.

Mary Taylor **£4.99**